Ben Franklin
and His First Kite

written by
Stephen Krensky

illustrated by
Bert Dodson

WITHDRAWN

Aladdin

New York London Toronto Sydney Singapore

First Aladdin edition June 2002

Text copyright © 2002 by Stephen Krensky

Illustrations copyright © 2002 by Bert Dodson

Aladdin Paperbacks

An imprint of Simon & Schuster

Children's Publishing Division

1230 Avenue of the Americas

New York, NY 10020

READY-TO-READ is a registered trademark of Simon & Schuster, Inc.

Also available in a Simon & Schuster Books for Young Readers edition.

The text for this book was set in 18 Point Century Old Style

Designed by Lisa Vega

The illustrations were rendered in water color

Printed in the United States of America

2 4 6 8 10 9 7 5 3 1

Cataloging-in-Publication Data available from the Library of Congress

ISBN 0-689-84984-2 (Aladdin pbk.)

ISBN 0-689-84985-0 (Aladdin Library Edition)

Ten-year-old Benjamin Franklin

was hard at work

in his father's candle shop.

He was cutting wicks.

He carefully laid out each one.

3

Ben stretched his arms
and let out a yawn.
Candles could be tall or short,
fat or thin,
and even different colors.
But there was nothing fun
about candles for Ben.

"When do you think
    we'll be done today?"
    Ben asked his father.
"Soon enough," his father answered.

"Why? Do you have special plans?"
Ben's father smiled.
It was a rare day indeed
when Ben did not have
a plan in mind.

"Yes," said Ben.

"I want to try an experiment
at the millpond."

"You'll be swimming, then?"
his father asked.

Ben grinned. "Partly," he said.

His father nodded.

Ben was a fine swimmer.

That afternoon Ben
flew down the streets of Boston.
He was headed for home.
Along the way he noticed the
waves cresting in the harbor.
The ships rocked back and forth.
That was good, he thought.
He needed a strong wind today.

When Ben got to his house,

his mother met him at the door.

Inside, two of his sisters

were busy making

hasty pudding by the hearth.

Ben had sixteen brothers and sisters.

"Ben," his mother said,

"why are you in such a hurry?"

Ben told her about his plan.

"Since your father approves,
I won't keep you,"
said his mother.
"Just be back for supper."
Ben nodded.
He ran to get the kite
he had made the week before.
Then he left the house.

At the millpond
a few of Ben's friends
had arrived to watch.
"You've picked a poor place
to fly a kite," said one.
Ben shrugged.
"I'm doing an experiment," he said.

Ben got undressed.

He gave his clothes

to one of his friends.

"Please carry these

to the other side

of the pond," he said.

"What are you going to do?"

asked the other boys.

"Carry the kite while you swim?"

"No," said Ben.

"The kite is going

to carry me."

"But that kite's nothing special.
It's just paper, sticks, and string,"
said one boy.
"That's true," Ben said.
"But you see,
the kite isn't the invention.
The invention is what
I'm going to do with it."

Ben raised the kite in the air.

Once the wind had caught

and carried it aloft,

Ben walked into the water.

There he lay on his back, floating.

"I'm going to cross this pond without swimming a stroke," said Ben.

The wind tugged on the kite.

The kite string tightened.

The water began

to ripple at Ben's feet.

The kite was pulling him!

The boys whooped
and hollered as Ben
glided across the pond.
Finally he reached the other side.
The other boys met him there.
"That was amazing!" said one.
"You crossed the whole pond
without swimming a stroke,"
said another.

28

29

"What will you do next?"

they asked.

"Another invention?"

"A different experiment?"

Ben didn't know.

But he was sure he would think

of something.

This book is based on a story about Benjamin Franklin. The timeline below identifies important events in his life.

1706	Born on January 17, the fifteenth of seventeen children
1716	Goes to work in his father's chandlery at age 10
1718	Becomes apprentice to his brother James
1723	Runs away from Boston for Philadelphia
1729	Buys the *Pennsylvania Gazette*
1730	Marries Deborah Read (has three children)
1732	Begins to print *Poor Richard's Almanack*
1740	Invents Pennsylvania fireplace, later called Franklin Stove
1752	Flies kite in thunderstorm to show that lightning is a form of electricity
1775	Joins the Second Continental Congress
1776	Helps draft and signs the *Declaration of Independence*
1776	Becomes American representative to France
1783	Helps negotiate Treaty of Paris
1790	Dies in Philadelphia on April 17